Searching

Catherine Haworth

BookLeaf
Publishing
India | USA | UK

Presentation by *BookLeaf Publishing*

Web: www.bookleafpub.com

E-mail: info@bookleafpub.com

ISBN: 9789357446112

First edition 2022

DEDICATION

To all girls across the world, still searching for themselves.

Autumn Days

Outside under the lowering sun,
She smiles sweetly as she plays.
Oblivious to the birds on the run -
She lifts her face towards the rays
Which dance across her cheeks with fun.
She enjoys the still-long days,
This time of year so heavenly
When the girl can still run free.

Some trees are glowing with green,
Yet ground littered with amber.
In order to appreciate the scene,
The branches she could clamber.
But her Mother said stay where seen,
So the girl's mood is damper.
Desire to see the world up high -
Limited by Mother's eye.

Then something new the girl now sees:
An array of flowers grown.
Hydrangeas, Carnations, Calla Lilies,
More than she had ever known.
One bloom makes her jaw fall widely,
A beautiful seed was sown.
A rose by any other name…

The girl wants it all the same.

The rose lures the girl, come close by,
So the girl runs over quick.
She avoids the thorns so delicately,
Careful not to let it prick
Her fingers as she starts to pry
It from the ground. Such magic
That this glorious rose is hers -
Her young heart, so pure, now stirs.

The leaves now turn from green to red.
Mother yells "inside" so loud,
And so into the house the girl is led
As she holds the rose in hand.
She did not know the rose was dead.
None of this is what she'd planned.
How could things have changed so quickly?
The rose, to her, still pretty.

As she clutches the rose so tight,
Heavy tears spring to her eyes.
She's fallen victim to its thorny bite,
And cannot escape her cries.
She was the reason for this plight;
The reason the rose had died.
Though Mother did not say the same,
The girl knew she was to blame.

She refused to let Mother aid,
And watched the red blood soon flow.
She just lay in the bed that she had made,
And watched the dark river grow.
Her actions left her stung, afraid.
So young; how was she to know?
Unaware of her wrongdoing,
Whilst days were froing, toing.

The girl had just been having fun,
Enjoying the fading days.
But now with the so quickly setting sun,
She wanted to change her ways.
So she'd never do what she'd done,
And her rose could live, always.

Gone

The leaves curl and crisp,
Petals decay; painted black.
The world seems empty -
Besides the unearthly crack.

Now there's emptiness,
In the garden, in the trees.
No more flowers bloom,
There's no more green in the leaves.

Autumn leaves are brown,
But the girl's sky is so dark.
She was free outside,
Now her heart is a caged lark

Refusing to sing.
Refusing to live her life.
What's the point of it?
The girl is consumed by strife.

The petals wither;
The point of disappearance.
The girl cannot cope,
Remembering the sun dance.

The girl mourns her rose,
No other flower comes close!
She remains alone,
Sullen, struggling, and morose.

Mother at a loss.
As time has kept on passing
The girl is static.
Her body still, eyes glazing.

Lives in denial,
But nothing can stop the crack.
… Will still smell as sweet?
The girl just wants her rose back.

Holding things inside,
The girl is right on the brink
Of exploding now.
Far too many thoughts to think.

Instead it builds and
Builds, and she reels in the loss.
What can she do now?
Now that her sweet rose is lost?

Broken and distraught,
She longs for better times.
Before all of this,
And before her horrid crimes.

It's all gone, gone, gone,
And the girl can't stop her tears;
How can she go on
Surrounded by all her fears?

It is but a rose!
Her mother tries to repair
The girl's great sadness,
But she still drowns in despair.

A rose, just a rose,
There will be others in time.
But choose another,
Feels like the biggest crime.

It goes against all
Of her desires and her dreams.
She cannot do it.
The thought tears her at the seams.

Too much, the girl cries,
She sees no way to go on.
Yes, only a rose,
But it's her rose that is gone.

And gone, so quickly,
Compared to the length of time.
Her plans go to waste

As she descends past her prime.

The crack gets wider,
The walls bulge with the pressure.
Should she let it out?
Would it be her end? Her cure?

Loss; overwhelming,
Sudden and unexpected.
Too young for all of this.
Too young to comprehend it.

So much not yet said
And now nothing to be done.
The girl remains sad,
And her sweet rose is still gone.

Stolen Sonnet

As the leaves fall, and the girl still wallows,
In the loss she's suffered, she is shaken.
She has no strength to stop what follows -
All plans she had for life are taken.

She is consumed; smothered by grief,
When she thinks of her future, she does weep.
She was in no place to stop a thief
Who took what was hers and cut so deep.

She does not believe what has been stolen.
Too many cogs in a broken wheel.
Without her future, she is fallen.
Now she does not know how to feel.

Despite her not wanting to fall behind,
She could not be sure of her strength of mind.

Doubt the Season

Out of the window she glances,
Whilst bare trees perform dances.
The sky now starts turning black,
What if the leaves never come back?

She thought of the summers she'd seen
And this was normal; so it seemed.
But what if the world had gone off track?
What if the leaves just don't come back?

Of course they will, her Mother said,
Whilst tucking the girl into bed.
But no dream could now distract
The thought: is the world still intact?

From the trees, the leaves just fell,
So only time could surely tell.
Now some patience the girl must hack,
To see if the leaves do come back.

The evidence of leaves remain,
On the ground, but not the same.
Their luscious green they all lack,
How can she know that they'll be back?

Her own mind she starts to doubt;
There are things she knows not about
Such as how old trees, full of cracks,
Not long from now, grow fresh leaves back?

The next morning comes around,
The leaves are still painting the ground.
Patience she does surely lack
For she just wants her green leaves back.

They'll be back, she tells herself,
Putting her worry on the shelf.
But one question, her mind does rack:
What if the leaves never come back?

Reality May Turn

She questions what she burns,
Under the dark night sky.
Reality may turn.
She is struggling to learn
About this man, some 'guy' -
She questions what she burns.
Overwhelmed with concern,
As flames are rising high.
Reality may turn.
Her thoughts - hard to discern -
Haze is blurring her eye.
She questions what she burns.
The smoke's fingers seem to to yearn
For something out of sight.
Reality may turn.
Now all gone, not to return,
Or maybe that's a lie.
She questions what she burns;
Reality may turn.

Winter Nights

These dark nights start so early,
And people shelter from the cold.
The girl's breath appears so curly,
As her words are being told.
A story saved for this time yearly,
A story passed from times of old.
The darkness causes her to shiver,
But her tale she must deliver.

These dark nights are oh, so chilly!
Especially for ones so young:
Little girls in dresses - frilly -
The innocence in old songs sung.
Little boys all acting silly,
Whose small necks were often wrung
For running and fooling around,
And pinching things they often found

In pockets of the tall and rich,
Too proud to look toward the ground,
As these children weren't those which
The noble would pay to have around.
They belonged in the gutter, in a ditch,
And moved only when their bodies found.
For these were the children of the streets,

Who fought and stole for all their treats.

Out of houses they had been thrown,
By people they had never met.
Now with no parents of their own,
These strangers say: that's what you get.
Away from everything they'd known,
But somehow they would not let
This dampen or dark their young souls,
Even out there in the cold.

Out they'd go, under cover of dark,
To find a source of livelihood.
They'd follow strangers in the park,
Knowing they were up to no good.
As a group, they'd plan each mark,
And each child knew where they stood.
As a team they'd work together,
A makeshift family, bonded forever.

These cold nights can be so cruel,
But the children still have to eat.
So they take the adults for a fool,
And swap their goods for bread and meat.
Their deft fingers are a tool,
Pinching things from those they greet.
The girl thought of the hardships faced,
By those, these streets had been graced.

Unfortunately, there were some nights,
Colder than anyone could bear.
Mornings brought such horrid frights,
When children's eyes could only stare.
Such horror with the morning lights -
If only this tragedy was rare…
So maybe do not look away,
In winter, spring or present day.

For once those girls wore pretty dresses,
And boys could innocently play.
Treated worse, the girl confesses,
Than any criminal or stray.
No longer princes or princesses,
Instead they clean chimneys all day.
So raise a glass, up, out your seats!
And praise the orphans of the streets.

Too Many

Too many thoughts
Spinning round her head,
This time of year
She always dreads.

Full of memories
Painful in her heart,
All those years,
But now apart.

The darkness falls,
Lingers too long.
A heavy shroud
Making her feel wrong.

It feels like lead
Weighing her down.
She must escape -
Or surely drown.

But no lifeguard
Is to be found.
Everyone gone -
No one around.

This winter darkness
Goes on and on.
She tries to survive,
Though all hope seems gone.

Maybe one day
She will stand tall.
But with this weight,
She can only fall.

Sharing

Darkness.
Temptation.
So many thoughts of frustration.
One of us.
All of them.
So many stories of mayhem.
Sharing.
Comparing.
"Look at what she's wearing!"
Childish.
Grown up.
The girl's half empty cup,
Draining,
Worsening.
All these images threatening
Young girls,
Any one,
Soon innocence is gone.
Sharing.
Daring.
Too many people not caring.
Give in.
Fly away.
They'll find another anyway.

Nature Denied

Mirror reflects not
What society desires.
Though try as she might.

One Step

The girl stands afraid.
One step forward,
One step back.
Heart pounding hard
Against her ribs;
They could crack.
Emotions flying,
Gap gets smaller.
Prepared for - thwack.
She wasn't ready,
Now in shock.
Should she pack
And leave, escape, run?
Everything she'd known,
Thrown off track.
Tears and never agains
Flood into her ears,
But they lack
The feelings needed
For the girl to be sure
Things could go back
To how they were -
Happiness and love
In a stack
Of wonderful memories,

Now infected with
A trojan hack.
But from now until the next;
One step forward,
One step back.

That Time of Year

Dead as a doornail, she thought,
As she glanced out across the garden.
The skeletons cast their shadows,
As the sun turned into the moon.
Small electric icicles
All hanging along the rooftops,
Became the only source of light
In the ever-lengthening evenings.
The glowing blues and greens
Made the branches seem so twisted.
Something once in beautiful bloom
Now withered into brittle bark.
The girl was scared by these
Strangers that stood outside.
They linger like the carolers,
Who attempt to bring some cheer.
But darkness changes key,
And the night brings minor
Details that turn the world
Into the winter unknown.
The tree inside is no better
As it towers over the room.
No amount of lights or tinsel,
Could make her feel at ease.
So may things to smile about,

And take joy in those around.
But something just wasn't right;
All bottled up inside.
She leans against the window frame,
And watches the pretty snowflakes fall.
A frozen carpet covers the ground,
Keeping the flowers deep in their graves.
Families gather around the fire,
But the girl has no flaming hearth
To bring brightness and warmth
In a chilling, endless night.
Stockings hang upon the wall,
But the girl just sees the empty space -
The place that once was full,
Now never would be again.
Loved ones passing gifts,
Ribbons decorating the floor.
Though so many toys are left,
Untouched to gather dust.
The gentle smell of gingerbread,
Mixed with cinnamon and regret.
So many things had not been said,
And now there wouldn't be a chance.
Lots of food is eaten,
And the crackers all get pulled.
The girl, so suddenly overwhelmed,
Tries to rest her weary head.
A silent night, a lifeless night,
The girl wishes she'd find joy

In this day so greatly celebrated,
And one that used to be so pure.
She tried to turn her mind
Back to happier years.
Those times were gone; things had changed,
And the girl was overcome
With a hollowness so heavy
That she worried for her heart.
Maybe it would collapse, or
The world would come crashing down.
She threw her hands up in the air,
With frustration and grief.
Why could she not be an elf,
And spend her time making toys.
Instead she was only here
To watch the world pass by.
Just hoping, dreaming, praying,
That things would change next year.

Spring Mornings

The air still crisp and chill
As the sun just starts to rise.
Light seeping through will
Set off the cockeral's cries.
For now everything is still,
As the sleeping dog lies.
But soon things will awaken,
And winter soon forsaken,

Frost becoming dew,
Plants begin to grow.
The sun starts shining through,
And green begins to show.
The leaves are back; it's true!
And frozen streams now flow.
The girl smiles when she sees,
The forest for the trees.

Pink blossoms bloom,
Scattered on the trees,
Somehow lifting gloom,
In all the girl sees.
Everything still looms,
Hope; difficult to foresee.
But she tries to stay strong

As time moves along.

As the hours pass,
And the sun rises high,
The sheep start to amass,
Newborn lamb legs try
To walk along the grass,
As the day passes by.
The sky a clearer blue -
She saw the world anew.

Birds spread their wings
As they flock to return.
The silent, spring bell rings,
A signal the birds learn
That the change of season brings
When the weather starts to turn.
The girl loves to watch them fly,
In their formations in the sky.

So many sounds of life
Fill the new spring air,
Cutting the breeze like a knife,
As it whispers at her hair.
No more worry, no more strife,
She thinks, under the sun's glare.
It is time for a fresh start;
It's time to figure out her part

In this world once so dark,
The sun now shows its face.
And in the darkness, lights a spark,
That the girl can seek to embrace.
Her garden, recently so stark
Now has flowers in its grace.
She wonders if this could truly be,
That spring could set her free.

Moving forward; now's the time,
The girl starts to believe.
Heading now towards her prime,
No longer time to grieve.
She can leave the cold behind,
And grow with her green leaves.
The girl is sure this morning -
That hope comes with the spring.

Poem 13

How can she smile?
It was only a short while
Ago that everything
Had come crashing
Down around her.

Time can heal,
But she doesn't feel
Like there is a way
To get through each day
Without the sun.

The new year begins.
Her heart still sings
The saddest song
As time moves along -
A ruined melody.

Laughing with friends,
But her heart still mends
Itself each day.
Pain not gone away.
She still feels broken.

The weight still heavy.

Her mind pays a levy
On the memories
In all she sees
Surrounding her.

Still so unsure.
There's no quick cure
For feelings like this;
The decimated bliss
She now lives in.

How can she go on?
The dark days are gone
And spring brings hope
Which could could help her cope
With life's misery.

Impatient

She dreams of reaching high,
Not knowing she could fall.

She has always wanted to fly,
And be the belle of the ball.

She lets out an impatient sigh,
As she tries to stand so tall.

She feels like she could cry,
As time continues to crawl.

She wants things to rush by,
So she can make the call.

She doesn't know that it's a lie.
She doesn't know about the wall.

She does not yet know why,
She cannot have it all.

Equality for All

Everyone deserves to feel
Qualms not brushed under the rug,
Ushered away just like a bug,
Against which some people do reel,
Like it's *their* rights which they steal.
Inequality is like a drug
That digs a hole which should not be dug,
Yearning for a chance to heal.
From now until the end of time,
One people we should see.
Rights for all, we should agree;
All being everyone.
Let's rid the world of grime,
Let the hatred now be gone.

Step by Step

Up the ladder,
She must climb,
Step by step,
Rhyme by rhyme.
To reach the top
She does stress
Of how on earth
She can progress.
Looking up
To clear blue sky,
She wonders when
She can fly.
Just remember,
There is time -
Step by step,
Rhyme by rhyme.

Summer Afternoons

The heat glistens across her skin
As she lies out on the sand.
But her mind turns within
Casting back to times less grand.
Times full of darkness and sin,
And things she doesn't understand.
She wants to enjoy the afternoon,
Before the sun turns to the moon.

She glances out across the sea,
Focusing on the gentle wave,
And all the green she could see
In the leaves that she would crave.
But something would not let her be;
To the seasons she was a slave.
Although the sun shines out so hot,
The winter dark is not forgot.

She had always loved the sun,
And the long summer days.
She joined in with all the fun,
And followed the holiday craze.
But now a new era had begun,
And summer had changed its ways.
For though she smiled when summer came,

The seasons continued with their game.

Passing, passing, time goes by.
The cold gets warm; the sun gets cold.
So many changes in the sky,
A story from the times of old.
Though never really explained why,
The seasons change as foretold.
So many things not understood,
So unsure if she ever would.

She shook her head; must return,
To the current moment of life.
Then from now she must discern
In order to escape her strife.
She should push away her concern,
And stop her fear running rife.
Instead she should bask in the sun,
See that life has just begun.

The girl is still so young,
With many years ahead.
Maybe the sad song she sung,
Can now be put to bed.
She can step up another rung
Of the ladder which does thread
Her life together.
She now could weather

Any storm if she so chose,
As she moves forward.
Healing as she grows,
Whilst moving onward
And upward, she knows
As she looks at her orchard
Of beautiful flowers and leaves;
She has everything still up her sleeve.

She can leave the dark behind
And take in the summer light.
Hope she may surely find,
Even when the day turns to night.
Maybe the world could be kind,
And one day she could stop the fight.
For now she'll rest her mind,
And leave the darkness far behind.

Summer Alone

Summer alone.
Not coming home.
She still struggles daily.
Sweltering heat,
She cannot beat,
As she spends summer alone.
Garden blooming,
Mind glooming,
In the summer heat.
Flowers glowing,
Trees are growing,
The outdoors really blooming.
Moving on.
Darkness gone.
Her heart is now glowing.
Step outside,
No more to hide,
As she carries on.

Family

Family is there
Through the summers and the falls.
Beautiful and pure.

All Are Stars

She, he, him,
Her, they, them.
Everyone can love,
Even if no glove
Has been made to
Fit what you do.
The girl can see
How all should be
Treated with kindness,
Instead of blindness,
To who people are,
As all are stars
In their own sky.

Meditation

The girl breathes deeply,
In and out.
Focusing her mind.

When her thoughts wander,
In and out,
She must re-centre.

Each breath brings peace,
In and out.
She hopes it will last forever.

She can do anything -
In and out -
That she puts her mind to.

The girl has now chosen,
In and out,
That she should come first.

For then she can really be,
In and out,
Happy and truly free.

www.ingramcontent.com/pod-product-compliance
Lightning Source LLC
La Vergne TN
LVHW041246200726
843507LV00013B/2828